DOG ON A LOG™
Let's GO! Books
Step 5

DOG ON A LOG Books
Tucson, Arizona

Public Domain images from
www.clker.com

ISBN: 978-1949471618

www.dogonalogbooks.com

DOG ON A LOG
Parent and Teacher Guides

General Information on Dyslexia and Struggling Readers

The Author's Routine for Teaching Reading

Book 1. *Teaching a Struggling Reader: One Mom's Experience with Dyslexia*

Book 2. *How to Use Decodable Books to Teach Reading*

Available for free from many online booksellers or read at:
www.dogonalogbooks.com/free

Download DOG ON A LOG printable gameboards, games, flashcards, and other activities at:
www.dogonalogbooks.com/printables.

Parents and Teachers:
Receive email notifications of new books and printables. Sign up at:
www.dogonalogbooks.com/subscribe

BAKE A CAKE

A companion to
BAKE A CAKE Chapter Book

DOG ON A LOG Let's GO! Books
Step 5

By Pamela Brookes

"Jan, do you want to help me bake a cake?" Mom asks. "The stuff for the cake is on the shelf."

"We must have eggs for the cake. Go get eggs from Pine Cone the hen," Mom says.

An egg drops at the gate. It broke. The hens want it for lunch.

"We will make the cake from nuts. We must crush the nuts," says Mom.

Mom puts the cake in to bake. When the bell rings it will be time to check the cake.

Mom gets red pads to lift the pan from the rack.

She sets the pan on a plate.

Kate Tate is in bed. She fell and broke her hip.

Jan, Mom, and Kate Tate have cake. Kate Tate smiles. Jan is glad that she and Mom made Kate Tate a cake.

Almond Orange Cake with Chocolate Chips Recipe

NUT ALLERGIES:
You can substitute 6 oz ground shelled raw unsalted pumpkin seeds and 1/2 cup ground flax seeds for the almond flour.

Ingredients:
14 ounces Clementines or Oranges
6 large Eggs (2 ounces each)
1/3 cup Honey
2 cups Almond Flour
1 ½ tsp Baking Powder
1/2 tsp Salt
1 1/3 cups Chocolate Chips (optional)

Directions:

Wash then boil the clementines or oranges until they are soft when pierced by a fork. This can take anywhere from 30 to 90 minutes depending on the size of the fruit. Allow the oranges to cool. Blending hot oranges with eggs could cause the eggs to change consistency.

Preheat oven to 300 degrees. Cut a piece of parchment paper about 7 1/2" x 8 ¾." Lightly oil the inside of a cast iron or glass bread pan. Place parchment paper so it covers the long sides and bottom of the bread pan.

Place the boiled oranges, eggs and honey in a blender and blend until smooth. Mix the Almond Flour, Baking Powder, and Salt in a batter bowl. Add the mixture from the blender and stir until smooth. Add in the chocolate chips and stir until the chips are evenly distributed.

Scoop the batter into the prepared bread pan being careful not to get the batter between the parchment and the pan. Carefully jiggle the pan so the batter completely fills the corners and there are no air pockets and the top of the batter is level and smooth. You may want to place a few chocolate chips on top in a decorative fashion.

Bake for 30 minutes then lightly cover the pan with a piece of foil, parchment, or silicone. If you placed chocolate chips on top of the batter, be careful to not smash the chips. If you use foil you can make a tent that raises a bit above the pan.

Bake for another 45-60 minutes or so until a baking thermometer inserted into the middle of the loaf reads about 205 to 210. Because this is a moist cake I like to get it closer to 210 degrees. Total baking time will be about to 1 hour 15 minutes to 1 ½ hours. This is a dense cake so baking can take a while. Remove and allow to cool. Remove loaf from pan, slice, and serve.

FOR A SWEETER CAKE use just 1 ½ cups almond flour or 4 oz ground pumpkin seeds and 1/3 cup ground flax. Reduce baking time to an hour or so.

Sight Words used in "Bake A Cake"

a, be, do, egg, eggs, for, from, go, have, her, is, me, puts, says, she, the, to, want, we, you

Approximately 135 words

DOG ON A LOG Books
Phonics Progression

DOG ON A LOG Pup Books
Book 1
Phonological/Phonemic Awareness:
- Words
- Rhyming
- Syllables, identification, blending, segmenting
- Identifying individual letter sounds

Books 2-3
Phonemic Awareness/Phonics
- Consonants, primary sounds
- Short vowels
- Blending
- Introduction to sight words

DOG ON A LOG Let's GO! and Chapter Books

Step 1
- Consonants, primary sounds
- Short vowels
- Digraphs: ch, sh, th, wh, ck
- 2 and 3 sound words
- Possessive 's

Step 2

- Bonus letters (f, l, s, z after short vowel)
- "all"
- −s suffix

Step 3

- Letter Buddies: ang, ing, ong, ung, ank, ink, onk, unk

Step 4

- Consonant blends to make 4 sound words
- 3 and 4 sound words ending in −lk, -sk

Step 5

- Digraph blend −nch to make 3 and 4 sound words
- Silent e, including "-ke"

Step 6

- Exception words containing: ild, old, olt, ind, ost

Step 7

- 5 sounds in a closed syllable word plus suffix -s (crunch, slumps)
- 3 letter blends and up to 6 sounds in a closed syllable word (script, spring)

Step 8

- Two-syllable words with 2 closed syllables, not blends (sunset, chicken, unlock)

Step 9

- Two-syllable words with all previously introduced sounds including blends, exception words, and silent "e" (blacksmith, kindness, inside)
- Vowel digraphs: ai, ay, ea, ee, ie, oa, oe (rain, play, beach, tree, pie, boat, toe)

WATCH FOR MORE STEPS COMING SOON

Let's GO! Books have less text

Chapter Books are longer

DOG ON A LOG Books
Sight Word Progression

DOG ON A LOG Pup Books
a, does, go, has, her is, of, says, the, to

DOG ON A LOG Let's GO! and Chapter Books

Step 1
a, and, are, be, does, go, goes, has, he, her, his, into, is, like, my, of, OK, says, see, she, the, they, to, want, you

Step 2
could, do, eggs, for, from, have, here, I, likes, me, nest, onto, or, puts, said, say, sees, should, wants, was, we, what, would, your

Step 3
as, Mr., Mrs., no, put, their, there, where

Step 4
push, saw

Step 5
come, comes, egg, pull, pulls, talk, walk, walks

Step 6
Ms., so, some, talks

Step 7
Hmmm, our, out, Pop E., TV

Step 8
Dr., friend, full, hi, island, people, please

More DOG ON A LOG Books

Most books available in Paperback, Hardback, and e-book formats

DOG ON A LOG Parent and Teacher Guides

Book 1 (Also in FREE e-book and PDF Bookfold)
- Teaching a Struggling Reader: One Mom's Experience with Dyslexia

Book 2 (FREE e-book and PDF Bookfold only)
- How to Use Decodable Books to Teach Reading

DOG ON A LOG Pup Books
Book 1
- Before the Squiggle Code (A Roadmap to Reading)

Books 2-3
- The Squiggle Code (Letters Make Words)
- Kids' Squiggles (Letters Make Words)

DOG ON A LOG Let's GO! and Chapter Books

Step 1
- The Dog on the Log
- The Pig Hat
- Chad the Cat
- Zip the Bug
- The Fish and the Pig

Step 2
- Mud on the Path
- The Red Hen
- The Hat and Bug Shop
- Babs the 'Bot
- The Cub

Step 3
- Mr. Bing has Hen Dots
- The Junk Lot Cat
- Bonk Punk Hot Rod
- The Ship with Wings
- The Sub in the Fish Tank

Step 4
- The Push Truck
- The Sand Hill
- Lil Tilt and Mr. Ling
- Musk Ox in the Tub
- The Trip to the Pond

Step 5
- Bake a Cake
- The Crane at the Cave
- Ride a Bike
- Crane or Crane?
- The Swing Gate

Step 6

- The Colt
- The Gold Bolt
- Hide in the Blinds
- The Stone Child
- Tolt the Kind Cat

Step 7

- Quest for A Grump Grunt
- The Blimp
- The Spring in the Lane
- Stamp for a Note
- Stripes and Splats

Step 8

- Anvil and Magnet
- The Mascot
- Kevin's Rabbit Hole
- The Humbug Vet and Medic Shop
- Chickens in the Attic

Step 9

- Trip to Cactus Gulch 1: The Step-Up Team
- Trip to Cactus Gulch 2: Into the Mineshaft
- Play the Bagpipes
- The Hidden Tale 1: The Lost Snapshot

All chapter books can be purchased individually or with all the same-step books in one volume.

Steps 1-5 can be bought as Let's GO! Books which are less text companions to the chapter books.

All titles can be bought as chapter books.

WATCH FOR MORE BOOKS COMING SOON

How You Can Help

Parents often worry that their child (or even adult learner) is not going to learn to read. Hearing other people's successes (especially when they struggled) can give worried parents or teachers hope. I would encourage others to share their experiences with products you've used by posting reviews at your favorite bookseller(s) stating how your child benefitted from those books or materials (whether it was DOG ON A LOG Books or another book or product.) This will help other parents and teachers know which products they should consider using. More than that, hearing your successes could truly help another family feel hopeful. It's amazing that something as seemingly small as a review can ease someone's concerns.

DOG ON A LOG Quick Assessment

Have your child read the following words. If they can't read every word in a Step, that is probably where in the series they should start. Get a printable assessment sheet at: www.dogonalogbooks.com/how-to-use/ assessment-tool/

Step 1
fin, mash, sock, sub, cat, that, Dan's

Step 2
less, bats, tell, mall, chips, whiff, falls

Step 3
bangs, dank, honk, pings, chunk, sink, gong, rungs

Step 4
silk, fluff, smash, krill, drop, slim, whisk

Step 5
hunch, crate, rake, tote, inch, mote, lime

Step 6
child, molts, fold, hind, jolt, post, colds

Step 7
strive, scrape, splint, twists, crunch, prints, blend

Step 8
finish, denim, within, bathtub, sunset, medic, habit

Step 9
hundred, goldfinch, free, wheat, inhale, play, Joe

CPSIA information can be obtained
at www.ICGtesting.com
Printed in the USA
LVHW042044130723
752187LV00035B/92

9 781949 471618